W9-ACJ-632

OUR BODIES

THE SKELETON AND MUSCLES

Steve Parker

Raintree

Chicago, Illinois

Titles in the series:
The Brain and Nervous System • Digestion
The Heart, Lungs, and Blood • Reproduction
The Senses • The Skeleton and Muscles

© 2004 Raintree

Published by Raintree, a division of Reed Elsevier, Inc.

Chicago, Illinois

Customer Service 888-363-4266, or visit our website at www.raintreelibrary.com

All rights reserved. No part of this book may be reproduced or utilized in any form or by any means, electronic or mechanical, including photocopying, recording, or by any information storage and retrieval system, without permission in writing from the publisher. Inquiries should be addressed to:

Copyright Permissions, Raintree, 100 N. LaSalle, Suite 1200, Chicago, IL 60602

Library of Congress Cataloging-in-Publication Data:

Parker, Steve.
  The skeleton and muscles / Steve Parker.
    p. cm. -- (Our bodies)
Includes bibliographical references and index.
Contents: The skeleton -- Inside bones -- The growing skeleton (case study) -- Bones of the skull and face -- Healthy bones (focus on health) -- The muscle system -- More muscles -- Tendons -- Inside a muscle -- Making movements (case study) -- Controlling muscles -- Muscles of the face and head -- Bone and muscle disorders (focus on health) -- How joints work -- Keeping joints healthy (case study) -- How the hands work -- The shoulder and arm (case study) -- The leg and foot -- The back joints and muscles -- Joint problems.
  ISBN 0-7398-6622-2 (lib. bdg.)
  1. Musculoskeletal system--Juvenile literature. [1. Muscular system.
2. Skeleton.] I. Title. II. Series.
  QP301.P3516 2004
  612.7--dc21
                        2003006594

Codman Sq. Branch Library
690 Washington Street
Dorchester, MA 02124-3511

JUN - - 2006

Picture Acknowledgments
Front Cover (main), pp.33 (b), 39, 45 Getty Images: front, 39 (Taxi), 33 (stone), 45 (Image Bank); front cover (inset), p.37 (right) Corbis Digital Stock; pp.1, 23 (top), 29, 40 Digital Vision; pp.4, 14, 15, 17, 19 (b), 20, 21, 26, 38, 44 Science Photo Library: 4 (Simon Fraser), 14 (NASA), 15 (Athenais, ISM), 17, 19 (Pr. S Cinti/CNRI), 20 (BSIP Ducloux), 21 (Astrid & Hanns-Frider Michler), 26 (Deep Light Productions), 38 (Salisbury District Hospital), 44 (Princess Margaret Rose Hospital);pp. 5, 30 Corbis: p.5 (Robbie Jack), p.30 (Steve Prezant); pp.7, 23 (b) Robert Harding Picture Library (Tony Gervis); pp.9, 13, 34–35 Alamy; p.11 Panos; pp.24, 31, 37(l) ImageState; p.35 FLPA (Chris Mattison); p.43 Wellcome Trust.

Printed and bound in Italy.
1 2 3 4 5 6 7 8 9 0
08 07 06 05 04

CONTENTS

INTRODUCTION

Supporting parts

Many parts of the body are soft and flexible—the nerves and brain, heart and blood vessels, stomach and intestines are all squishy and bendable. The body is held up by a very strong set of supporting parts called bones. Each bone is rigid and strong, and all the bones together form the body's inner framework, which allows us to stand tall and move around.

Between bones

Bones are not separate parts, distant from one another and scattered around the body. They are linked together at joints of many different sizes and designs. Joints hold the bones together so they do not come apart, and they let bones move in relation to one another. Joints also reduce wear and tear, stopping the ends of the bones from rubbing and scraping against one another as they move back and forth.

The body's inner supporting framework, called the **skeleton,** shows up clearly in this whole-body scan as pale white-pinkish bones of many sizes and shapes.

Pulling bones

Bones cannot move by themselves.
They are moved by muscles. The body
has hundreds of muscles, ranging from
large and powerful ones, like those in
the hips and upper legs, to tiny and
delicate muscles deep inside the ear.
Muscles have two main tasks: to get
shorter, or **contract,** and to get longer
or **relax.** Most muscles are firmly joined
to bones. As a muscle contracts, it pulls
on the bones and moves them nearer to

Dancers train to ensure that their muscles are strong and their
joints are flexible, so that they can take up hundreds of
different body positions.

one another. This is how body parts
move. The muscles, bones, and joints
make up the musculoskeletal system.
This system supports us and enables us
to walk, jump, run, lift, and pull objects.
It also allows us to smile, shout, clap,
and even breathe.

THE SKELETON

In the middle

If you were to take away a body's skin, nerves, blood vessels, muscles, guts, and other soft parts, the last items left, in the middle of the body, would be the bones. The adult human body has a total of 206 bones, and together they are known as the **skeleton.** Bones make up about one-sixth of the body's total weight.

Rib cage

Vertebral column

Front and rear views of the skeleton look different, especially the skull and vertebral column of backbones.

Hip bone (pelvis)

Base of vertebral column (sacrum)

Shin bone (tibia)

Calf bone (fibula)

Busy bones

Old bones and skeletons in museums and exhibitions usually look dry, dull, flaky, yellowed, and brittle. But inside the body, living bones are very different. They are grayish and damp looking, slightly bendable, and very much alive. Like other body parts, they have blood vessels and nerve connections. They even change shape slowly and slightly through life, in

ANIMAL VERSUS HUMAN

Sharks are powerful hunters of the open ocean. Like us, they have a skeleton—but there is not a single bone in a shark's body. Its skeleton is made entirely of cartilage rather than bone.

response to stresses and strains on the body and its patterns of movement. This can happen when someone changes from one sport or activity to another, for example, switching from swimming to dancing.

Names of bones

Every bone has a scientific or medical name. In fact, every part of every bone—each lump or bump, hollow, or curve—has its own scientific name. Many bones also have more ordinary, everyday names. For example, the kneecap is known scientifically as the patella, and the cheekbone is called the zygomatic bone. The "funny bone" is not a whole bone; it is formed by the elbow ends of the long bones called the humerus in the upper arm and the ulna in the forearm.

Cartilage

Bone is the skeleton's main structural substance, and it is very strong. But the body has another structural substance called **cartilage.** Cartilage is similar in many ways to bone, but it is slightly softer and much more bendable. With bone, cartilage forms parts of the skeleton, especially in the ribs in the chest. Cartilage also covers the ends of bones in joints and makes up several structural parts of the body, such as the nose and ears.

Try this!

If you press your nose or tweak your ear, it bends. They have cartilage inside, to support them and give them shape. If they were bone, they would be very stiff. Knocked hard, they might snap off.

INSIDE BONES

Layer upon layer

A bone is like a piece of wood—light, tough, hard, strong, and slightly bendable. But unlike wood, bone is not the same all the way through. Most bones have three layers, one inside the other.

Outer covering
(periosteum)

Blood supply
to bone

A typical bone has three main layers—a hard outer shell or casing of compact bone, a spongy layer under this, and a center of jelly-like marrow.

End or head
of bone

Compact
(hard) bone

Cancellous
(spongy)
bone

Marrow
and blood
vessels

Main length or
shaft of bone

On the outside

The outer layer of bone is known as **compact bone,** or hard bone. It provides most of the toughness and strength. Compact bone is made of thousands of tiny rod-shaped parts called osteons, which are tightly packed together. Each osteon is thinner than a human hair and consists of layers of hard mineral crystals.

MICRO BODY

In each osteon, crystals and fibers are arranged in wider and wider layers, like smaller tubes inside larger tubes. In the hole along the middle are microscopic blood vessels and a tiny nerve.

The crystals, mainly **calcium, phosphate,** and carbonate, are scattered among bundles of threadlike fibers of another substance, the protein **collagen.**

In the middle

Inside compact bone is a layer of **cancellous bone,** or spongy bone. It is a mass of collagen fibers and mineral crystals, like compact bone, but it also contains thousands of small, bubble-like holes. Cancellous bone is strong and light. It helps to reduce the weight of the whole bone and allows it to be slightly flexible, so that under great stress, it is more likely to bend than it is to snap.

On the inside

Most bones have a soft, jelly-like center, called **bone marrow.** This center makes microscopic new red and white blood **cells** for the whole body's blood system. The new cells replace blood cells that naturally wear out and die. Bone marrow is very busy. The marrow in the body's bones makes two million new red cells and tens of thousands of new white cells every second.

ANIMAL VERSUS HUMAN

We have our bones on the inside. Some animals have bone on the outside, too. Tortoises, armadillos, and pangolins have body coverings made of bony plates for protection. The bone is covered by horn, another tough substance.

THE GROWING SKELETON

The unborn baby

Like other body parts, the bones of an unborn baby start to develop when it is tiny, hardly larger than your thumb. But at this very early stage, the "bones" are not actually made of bone. Their shapes form first as softer **cartilage.** Over months in the womb, and then in the years after birth, this cartilage gradually develops mineral crystals and hardens into true bone. This process is called ossification.

Stages of growth

The **skeleton** begins to appear in the form of cartilage by about the third week after a human body starts to

The changing size and proportions of the growing body are based on the developing skeleton. As a child grows, parts of the skeleton that first formed as cartilage turn into bone. One of the main changes is the formation of mineral crystals, such as **calcium** and **phosphate**, that make the bone harder but less flexible.

develop from the tiny fertilized egg inside its mother's womb. After another five weeks (which is still seven months before birth), some of this cartilage starts to harden into true bone as the skeleton continues to grow in size. This process happens at different rates in different areas of the body. When a baby is born, its skull and backbone are very well formed and hardened into bone, although they are still growing. The wrist and ankle "bones" have much less bone—they are still mainly cartilage. The long bones in the arms and legs will not be completely bone until 15–18 years of age, when the person reaches full adult height.

Bone problems

Bones need minerals and other substances to become tough and hard. One important substance is vitamin D. If this is lacking in a pers   harden
fully   bone problems   d grow
in th   appens
duri   eton is
grow   ts. It
can   bent or
"bowed" legs. The same problem in adults is known as osteomalacia.

Lack of the right foods makes the bones weak, so they cannot support the body and do not grow in the usual shape.

ANIMAL VERSUS HUMAN

Some animal skeletons develop very fast. A mouse's is fully grown by four weeks. Other animal skeletons never stop developing. A tortoise or crocodile may still be growing at 80 years old—although more slowly than when it was younger.

BONES OF THE SKULL AND FACE

Protection

The main bones inside the head are called the skull and lower jaw. The complicated shape of the skull protects five of the body's most delicate parts—the eyes, ears, and brain. The two eyes are set in deep bowls, called orbits, in the front of the skull. The tiny inner parts of each ear are inside a chamber within the thickness of the side of the skull, in the temporal bone. The brain is protected by the curved dome over the top, known as the cranium.

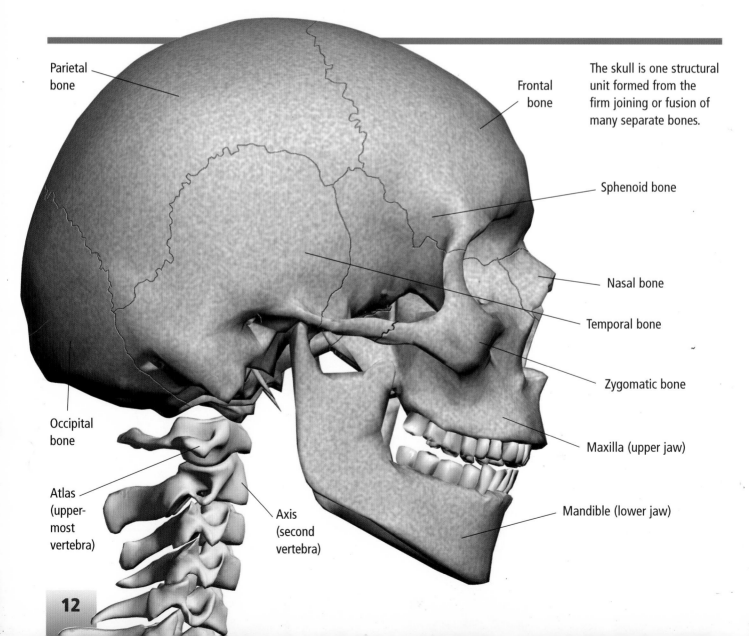

Parietal bone

Frontal bone

The skull is one structural unit formed from the firm joining or fusion of many separate bones.

Sphenoid bone

Nasal bone

Temporal bone

Zygomatic bone

Occipital bone

Maxilla (upper jaw)

Atlas (uppermost vertebra)

Axis (second vertebra)

Mandible (lower jaw)

The proportions of the skull bone determine the overall shape of the face, from wide to narrow.

The smallest bones

The human skull is made of 21 bones linked firmly at suture joints (see page 32). There are seven other bones in the head, too. Six of the bones (three are deep inside each ear) are the smallest bones of the entire body. They are the hammer, anvil, and stirrup. The stirrup is hardly larger than this letter U. These bones help us hear by passing sound vibrations from the eardrum to the innermost ear. The seventh bone is one of the body's strongest—the lower jaw, or mandible. It is moved by muscles that are, for their relative size, some of the body's most powerful. They are the temporalis in front of the ear and the masseter under the cheek bone. These are the muscles we use to bite and chew.

Top Tips

In risky sports and activities, a helmet, hard hat, or head guard protects not only your skull, but your eyes and ears—and your brain. In some high-speed activities, like skiing and bicycling, you cannot take part in official events unless you wear some form of protection on your head.

Try this!

Speak loudly as normal, then hold your nose and speak again. Your voice sounds different. Normally, sounds pass through the nose, and this is linked to air chambers called sinuses, which are inside the bones of your face. The sounds fill these air chambers and make your voice louder and clearer. If you hold your nose, air cannot pass this way.

HEALTHY BONES

Keeping fit

The body stays healthier and in better shape if it keeps active. This is true of all body parts, including bones. Every day, we can make sure that our bones and other body parts have the best chance of staying strong and healthy.

Eating and bones

Bones contain minerals such as **calcium** and **phosphate.** To keep our bones healthy, we need to eat plenty of these minerals in a range of foods, such as dairy products, meat, fish, and fresh fruits and vegetables. In an emergency, when food is lacking, the body can take some of the minerals out of the bones for more urgent needs elsewhere. But this weakens the bones, and the minerals need to be replaced quickly.

Activity and bones

If muscles are not used regularly, they become weak and gradually waste away. The same happens to bones. They are designed to cope with a certain amount of stress and strain during movement. Most kinds of activity keep bones strong and tough and benefit other body parts, like the heart and lungs.

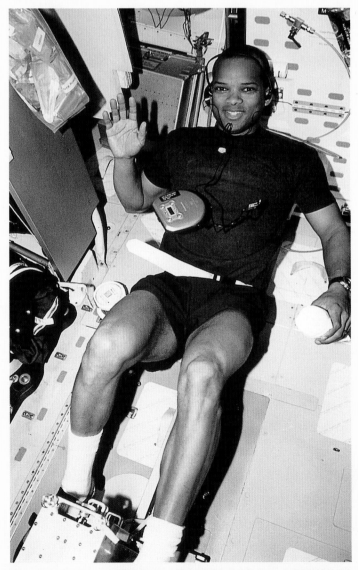

Astronauts need to get regular exercise, otherwise the weightless conditions of space would weaken their bones and muscles.

Activities range from energetic sports such as football and tennis, to swimming, jogging, and even brisk walking. Doing the opposite—sitting and lying down for long periods of time—means that bones lose their strength and become at greater risk for breaks or other injuries.

Helping bones

Bones are tough, but sometimes they are put under so much stress that they crack or even break. This usually happens when the body is moving fast and is stopped suddenly, as in a car accident, a fall, or a collision in high-speed sports. It's important to wear seatbelts and protective clothing and equipment. A helmet protects the skull. Shoulder pads cover the collar bones. Elbow and knee guards protect the bone ends and the joints there. In soccer, shin guards cover the front of the lower leg, which is at risk from the accidental kicks of other players.

This X ray shows a break (see upper left) in the fibula or calf bone, in the lower leg just above the ankle.

Try this!

Feel where bones are near the surface of the body. They form hard bumps just under the skin. Bones in these places are at risk of cracks or breaks when knocked hard, because they are not covered by softer parts like muscles or fat, which absorb the blow. Examples include the shin, ankle, elbow, and collar bone.

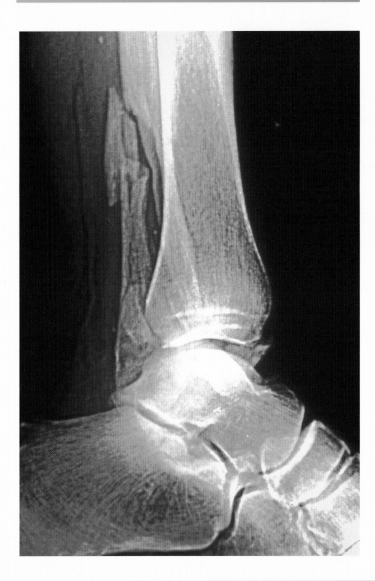

THE MUSCLE SYSTEM

Making movements

Muscles do almost nothing except **contract,** and then **relax** and become longer again. By doing this, they create every movement of the body. This includes not only the movements we see on the outside, such as walking, running, and jumping. It also includes movements inside the body, like swallowing, breathing, and pumping blood.

Biceps brachi

Triceps brachi

Flexors for fingers

Extensors for fingers

Gracilis

Gluteus maximus

Biceps femoris

Rectus femoris

Tibialis anterior

Gastrocnemius

Extensors for toes

Flexors for toes

Some of the main superficial, or outermost, muscles of the body.

Muscles and bones

The body has about 640 **skeletal muscles.** These are the muscles that are mainly joined to the bones of the **skeleton.** Skeletal muscles pull bones to move the body around. Skeletal muscles are also called voluntary muscles, because we can control them in a voluntary way (at will) by thoughts and decisions. They also are known as striped muscles, because under the microscope they have a pattern of tiny light and dark stripes. Other kinds of muscles, which are not voluntary and not striped, are shown on the next pages.

MICRO BODY

Skeletal or striped muscle shows its dark and light bands, or striations, under the microscope. As it gets shorter, the lighter bands become narrower. The striations (stripes) of skeletal muscle are formed by the overlapping of long, thin substances within them, especially **actin** and **myosin.**

Try this!

Instead of bones, wide sheets of muscles protect the front of the abdomen (belly or tummy). Tense and pull them in as if you are getting ready to blow out hard. Feel how they form a stiff, strong layer to protect the soft inner parts behind them.

Names and shapes

We often think of a muscle as long, bulging in the middle, and thinner at each end where it attaches to a bone. This is true for many muscles in the arms and legs. But there are other shapes of muscles. Sometimes a muscle's name is taken from its shape or its connections with bones. The deltoid muscle in the shoulder has three sides, like a triangle ("delta" means triangle shaped). The triceps muscle in the arm is named because it is Y-shaped with three ends, which are called "heads" in muscles ("tri" means three and "ceph" means head).

MORE ABOUT MUSCLES

Different types

Most of the muscles in the body are **skeletal muscles** (see previous page). They form about two-fifths of the body's weight. They pull on bones and move the body around, and we can control them at will. But the body has two other kinds of muscle, known as **visceral muscle** and **cardiac muscle.**

Esophagus

Windpipe (trachea)

Arteries (blood vessels)

Lung airways (bronchi)

Stomach

Intestines

Ureter (from kidney to bladder)

Tubes and tracts of reproductive parts

Muscles for the insides

Visceral muscle is found mainly as layers in the walls or coverings of inner body parts like the stomach and intestines, blood vessels, and air tubes in the lungs. It also forms baglike containers, such as in the bladder. Visceral muscle is sometimes called smooth muscle because under the microscope it does not have tiny stripes like skeletal muscle. It looks smooth and flat. Visceral muscle is also known as involuntary muscle. This is because it works automatically, on its own, and we cannot affect it at will by thinking.

Smooth (visceral or involuntary) muscle is found in many body parts, including the walls of blood vessels that branch throughout the body.

Visceral muscles are not joined to bones. They work by contracting in a wavelike fashion along their length. In a tube, this pushes the contents along. An example is in the intestine (gut), where food is pushed and squeezed along as it is digested. The wavelike squeezing motion is known as **peristalsis.**

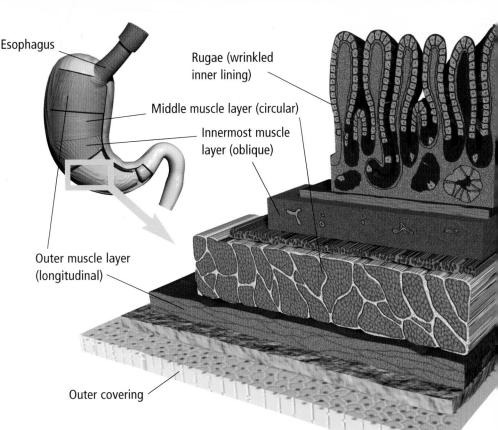

Esophagus

Rugae (wrinkled inner lining)

Middle muscle layer (circular)

Innermost muscle layer (oblique)

Outer muscle layer (longitudinal)

Outer covering

The stomach wall contains several layers of smooth muscle, which have their fibers arranged in different directions to allow a wide range of squeezing movements.

Heart muscle

The heart is almost all muscle—a special type called cardiac muscle or myocardium. The heart muscle is different because it is striped (like voluntary muscle) but it is involuntary (like visceral muscle). Skeletal muscles get tired or fatigued if we use them too much. Heart muscle never fatigues—which is lucky for us, because it has to contract and pump blood every second to keep the body alive.

Try this!

Swallow hard while touching your neck to feel the muscles of your esophagus inside your neck. They contract or squeeze like a wave, to push swallowed items down into your stomach.

MICRO BODY

Under a microscope, visceral muscle lacks the thin stripes or bands of skeletal muscle. It also can contract for longer periods than skeletal muscle can without getting tired. This is smooth or visceral muscle magnified 3,760 times.

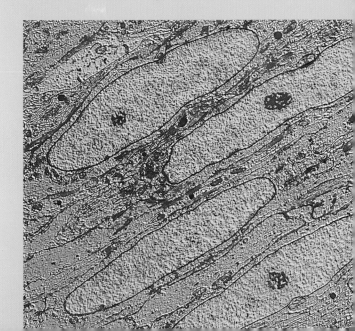

TENDONS

Anchored onto bones

A bulging muscle does not usually join directly to a bone. In most cases, the muscle end tapers into a tough, ropelike, narrow **tendon.** This is the part that is firmly stuck or anchored onto the bone. Tendons are pale because they have much less blood in them than muscles. They are made mainly of stringlike fibers of the body substance **collagen** (which is also found in bones and skin).

Living glue

At the muscle end, the tendon is joined mainly to the outer layer, or "skin" around the muscle, known as the epimysium. At the bone end, it is joined to a similar outer "skin" around the bone, called the periosteum. Both of these joints are very strong. It takes great force to pull a tendon from its bone or muscle, or to stretch it so that it tears. If this happens, we often call it a "strained muscle" or "torn muscle" but actually it's really the tendon that is injured.

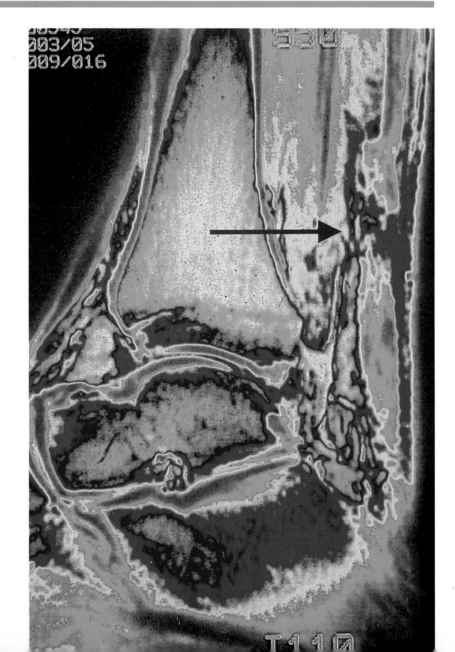

This computer-colored scan shows an Achilles tendon above a heel that was put under excessive strain, resulting in a tear (arrowed).

Long tendons

Some muscles have more than one "end."
When you curl up your toes, you use
a muscle in the front of the lower leg,
called an extensor. It has one tendon
at its upper end. At the lower end, it
branches into three parts, each with a
tendon. The three tendons run down
through the ankle and along the top of
the foot, to pull on the tops of the toes
and make them curl up.

Tendons are pale in color, partly because they
contain less blood than well-supplied, blood-rich
body parts such as muscles.

Try this!

Stand up straight, then bend your
knees to crouch slightly. Feel two large
tendons just above the back of your
knee, called hamstring tendons, take
the strain. Also feel the body's largest
tendon, just above the heel, called the
calcaneal or Achilles tendon.

MICRO BODY

This microscope view of a tendon shows
its strong, stringy fibers, which have few
blood vessels or nerves. The low blood
supply means an injured tendon usually
takes a long time to heal.

Muscle fibers

A big muscle contains thousands of long, thin parts called **muscle fibers** (myofibers). Each one of these is thinner than a human hair. In most muscles the fibers are about 2 inches (3 or 3 centimeters) long, but in a long muscle, they may be 14 inches (30 centimeters) long. The muscle fibers are wrapped in bundles known as fascicles, and the whole muscle is wrapped in a strong outer layer, or skin, called the epimysium (see page 20).

Bundle of muscle fibers (fascicle)

Outer covering (epimysium)

This view shows a muscle enlarged to reveal its fibers, which are magnified to show the fibrils.

Covering of bundle (perimysium)

Muscle fiber (myofiber)

Banding pattern or stripes on fibril

Fiber is bundle of muscle fibrils (myofibrils)

Muscle fibril is bundle of muscle filaments (myofilaments)

Top Tips

Muscles need energy to work. Blood brings sugars (from digested food) and **oxygen** (taken in by breathing) to the muscles. So exercise makes the lungs breathe faster, and the heart beat faster, too, supplying more blood so that the muscles can work harder.

Parts that pull

A single muscle fiber contains a bundle of even thinner parts, known as muscle fibrils (myofibrils). These have light and dark patches that line up across many fibrils, to give a striped or banded appearance (see page 17). The fibrils are made of two body substances, or proteins, known as **actin** and **myosin.** These are long and thin, lie alongside each other, and partly overlap. To make the muscle pull, the actins and myosins slide past each other so the whole fibril becomes shorter. Most muscles can contract to about two-thirds their length, bulging fatter as they do so.

In a muscle fibril, actins and myosins move past each other, like people pulling hand-over-hand on a rope.

ANIMAL VERSUS HUMAN

Some animals have far more muscle in their bodies for their size than we do. The gorilla is especially strong. It does not have more muscles than we do, but each muscle is bigger than the same muscle in a person. An adult male gorilla is more than one-half muscle.

MAKING MOVEMENTS

Working together

Very few movements in the body use just one muscle. If you bend your elbow, the main muscle involved is the biceps. You can see it bulging in the top of your upper arm. But under this are two more muscles, the coraco-brachialis near the shoulder and the brachialis lower down toward the elbow. These two help the biceps. At the same time, other muscles become tense all down your arm, from shoulder to wrist. Otherwise your shoulder would tilt forward, and your wrist and hand would be floppy. The "simple" movement of bending your elbow involves at least 20 muscles!

Hundreds of muscles all over the body are used when dancing to produce graceful, delicately controlled motions.

Try this!

Whirl your arm around at the shoulder like a windmill, and feel the wide range of movements at this joint. It involves at least 50 muscles, which pull or steady the arm in different ways as it goes around in a circle.

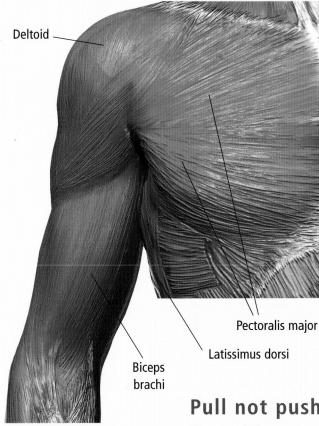

Deltoid

Pectoralis major

Latissimus dorsi

Biceps
brachi

Top Tips

Muscles help control the amount of movement in a joint, so the bones do not go too far and come apart. Joints should never be forced so that they become painful—pain warns of damage. However, gentle bending and flexing, gradually over a long period, helps joints to move farther and more easily.

The shoulder is surrounded and stabilized by many muscles, which move the upper arm and the elbow.

Pull not push

To straighten your elbow, you do not use the biceps again. A muscle can only pull. It cannot forcefully push to move bones farther apart. The elbow is straightened by the triceps muscle in the underside of your upper arm. As the triceps shortens, the biceps becomes **relaxed** or floppy, and the movement stretches it longer. So the biceps moves the elbow one way, and the triceps moves it back again. These two muscles are called opposing, or **antagonistic,** partners. Straightening the elbow, like bending it, uses a host of other muscles from the shoulder down to the wrist. Nearly all body movements are like this. They use teams of muscles, rather than just one or two.

Twin heads (upper ends) of biceps brachi

Biceps brachi

Triceps brachi

The triceps and biceps are opposing muscle partners. The biceps got its name because it has two ends, or heads, while the triceps has three.

CONTROLLING MUSCLES

Nerve messages

Skeletal or **voluntary muscles** do not move on their own. Otherwise our body actions would be very random, jerky, and clumsy. They are controlled by the brain. It sends out messages along nerves, which are like bendable wires that branch throughout the body. Nerve messages are tiny pulses of electricity. The nerve end passes the messages into the muscle fibers, to make these **contract.** Nerve messages travel very fast, at 328 feet (100 meters) per second or more. So a message's journey, from brain to muscle, takes a fraction of a second.

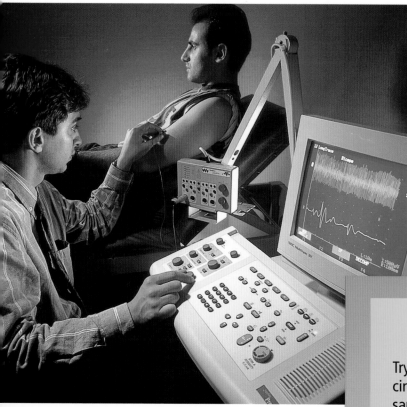

The tiny electrical signals made by active muscles are displayed by an electromyograph (EMG) machine.

Movements and the brain

The nerve messages to muscles come from several parts of the brain. The main one is the movement center, or motor cortex. This is a strip on the outside of the brain, from the top of the head, down toward the ear. It's the place where we think about and decide to make or stop voluntary movements.

Try this!

Try to pat your head with one hand, and rub circles on your stomach with the other, at the same time. It's very difficult at first because it is an unnatural movement that we rarely do. But keep practicing. The brain gradually learns to move the muscles in the right way.

Main part of brain (cerebrum)

After leaving the motor cortex, the nerve messages pass through another part of the brain before they leave along nerves. This is the small, wrinkled cerebellum, at the brain's lower rear.

The cerebellum "fills in the details" of exactly which muscles should contract, and when, and by how much. We are not usually aware of this. We decide in the motor cortex to make a movement and then go on to other thoughts. The cerebellum takes care of the details. It makes our movements smooth, practiced, and coordinated, and helps us to learn new ones, like playing a piano, rollerblading, or sewing.

Motor cortex

Cerebellum

Spinal cord

Motor nerve

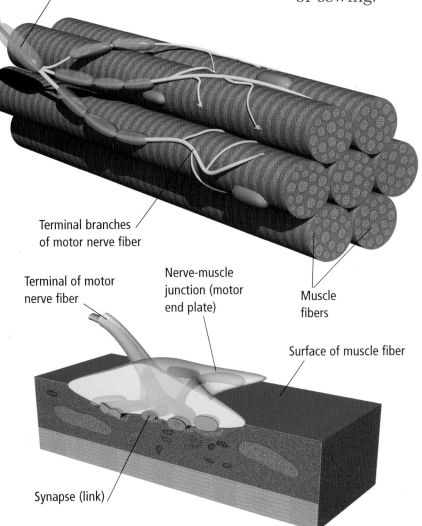

Terminal branches of motor nerve fiber

Terminal of motor nerve fiber

Nerve-muscle junction (motor end plate)

Muscle fibers

Surface of muscle fiber

Synapse (link)

Nerve messages from parts of the brain (top) travel along nerves to muscles (left), where the nerve endings are embedded in the hair-fine muscle fibers (bottom).

MICRO BODY

The motor end plate is a spiderlike, microscopic part that joins a nerve end to a muscle. It passes the nerve messages into the muscle fibers to make them contract.

MUSCLES OF THE FACE AND HEAD

Unusual and useful

Under the skin of the face, there are about 50 muscles. They are among the most unusual and useful in the body. They are unusual because some of them are not joined to bones at each end. They are joined to one another, by straps of fibers. They form a complex web or network of muscles, which can move in hundreds of different ways. These muscles give us a vast range of facial expressions, so we can communicate our thoughts and feelings to other people, without a sound.

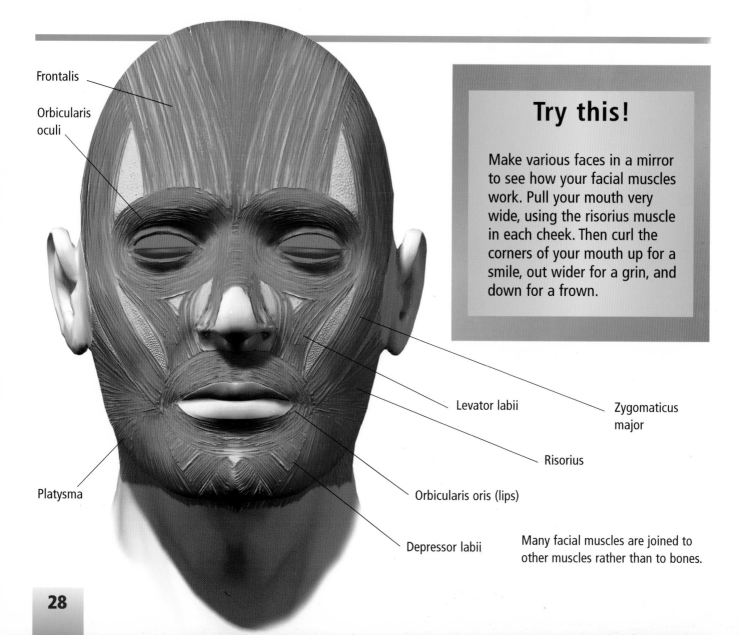

Frontalis

Orbicularis oculi

Platysma

Levator labii

Zygomaticus major

Risorius

Orbicularis oris (lips)

Depressor labii

Many facial muscles are joined to other muscles rather than to bones.

Try this!

Make various faces in a mirror to see how your facial muscles work. Pull your mouth very wide, using the risorius muscle in each cheek. Then curl the corners of your mouth up for a smile, out wider for a grin, and down for a frown.

Open and shut

Each eyelid is a four-part, circle-shaped muscle called the orbicularis oculi. It has a large opening in the middle that we see through. When this muscle **contracts,** the upper and lower parts come together to close the opening. This is how we blink our eyelids and shut our eyes. There is a similar but larger circlelike muscle in the lips, the orbicularis oris. When it contracts, the mouth closes.

Flexible muscle

The body's most flexible muscle is just behind the lips. It's the tongue. In fact, a tongue has 12 separate muscles. It is much longer in total than the part you can see. It is anchored at its lower end, down in the throat and neck region. The tongue can twist and curve into many shapes, from short and wide to long and thin. Using the tongue, we can eat, lick, swallow, suck, speak, and even whistle.

ANIMAL VERSUS HUMAN

Lizards do not seem to laugh or frown. In fact, they cannot, even if they wanted to. They have fewer and less complicated muscles in their faces. Only a few animals can make lots of facial expressions, mainly monkeys and apes.

The lips of a chimp are very flexible, and are able to make many facial expressions and gather small food items.

BONE AND MUSCLE DISORDERS

Injuries

Bones and muscles are the body's most physical parts, carrying out endless movements, often under stress and strain. Sometimes the stress becomes too much, and something "snaps."

A fracture is a crack, split, or complete break in a bone. As a bone heals after a break or fracture, microscopic cells in the bone form new fibers and mineral crystals. After a few months, the break is hardly visible. A dislocation is where two bones in a joint, which are supposed to be held next to each other, come completely away from each other. A sprained **ligament** is when the joint bones move farther from each other than they should and stretch or tear some of the muscle or ligaments.

Treatment

The usual treatment for these injuries is for a doctor to put all parts back in their correct places, with an operation if necessary. This is followed by resting the affected part, and then very gradual movements and some gentle exercises.

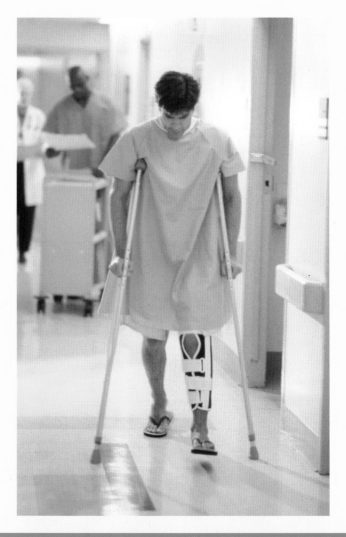

Crutches help to take the weight off an injured leg while it is exercised to keep it mobile.

Weak muscles

Compared with most other body parts, muscles do not suffer from many diseases. In paralysis, a body part cannot be moved. This is more often due to a problem in the brain or nerves that control a muscle rather than the muscle itself. In muscular dystrophy, the **muscle fibers** do not work properly because of a problem in the way they use the mineral **calcium,** which helps to control their contraction. The muscles become weak.

Weak bones

Because bones are the body's support system, any problem that reduces their strength can have widespread effects. In osteoporosis, bones lose their hard mineral structure and become weak, brittle, and crumbly. This condition tends to affect older women because their bodies have stopped producing certain natural body chemicals, or **hormones,** that help to keep bones strong. Osteoporosis is also made more likely by smoking, unhealthy eating with not enough **vitamins** and minerals, and lack of exercise. It can often be treated by medication and by gradual activity to strengthen the bones again.

Warming-up helps you determine if any parts need extra support.

Top Tips

In some sports and activities, special joint supports are recommended. These give extra support to certain joints that are at risk of coming apart or dislocating, because of the patterns of movement involved in the sport. Examples of supports include bandages, strappings, or lightweight plastic shields on the shoulders, elbows, wrists, knees, or ankles.

HOW JOINTS WORK

Where bones meet

A joint is a structure where two bones meet. Not all joints are flexible or allow the bones to move in relation to one another. In some parts, such as the skull, the individual bones are firmly linked, as if glued together. In other parts, such as the arms and legs, there are synovial joints that allow various amounts and directions of movements.

Fontanelles (gaps) in young skull

Sutures (firm joints) in adult skull

The bones of a baby's skull (top) gradually grow together at suture joints during childhood (above).

Fixed joints

The skull seems like one bone, but it is really made up of 21 bones, fixed to one another by rigid joints called suture joints. In a suture joint, tough fibers grow between the bones, along their edges, and then gradually shrink to pull the bones closer together. The fibers also become hardened by minerals, almost like regular bone. This whole process takes a year or two. A newborn baby's skull bones are not quite solid, and there are gaps between them, which the bones grow into. This structure allows the baby's head to get slightly smaller as it emerges from the womb along the narrow birth canal.

Flexible joints

In a synovial joint, such as the shoulder, the ends of the bones are covered with smooth, shiny, slightly soft cartilage. This allows the bones to slide past one another with minimal wear. A tough synovial capsule surrounds the joint like a bag. Its lining makes slippery

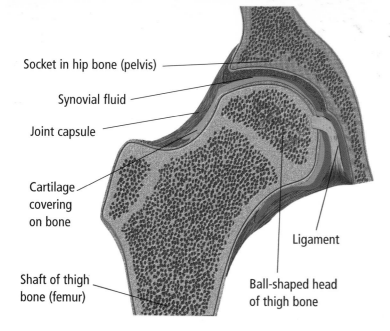

Socket in hip bone (pelvis)

Synovial fluid

Joint capsule

Cartilage covering on bone

Shaft of thigh bone (femur)

Ligament

Ball-shaped head of thigh bone

These views show the inside of the hip joint (left) and the ligaments and other coverings (below).

Hip bone (pelvis)

Ilio-femoral ligament

Pubo-femoral ligament

Shaft of thigh bone (femur)

synovial fluid.
Synovial fluid works like lubricating oil in a car's engine, so that the joint can move smoothly without rubbing or friction.

Ligaments

In a flexible joint, such as the knee, the bones are held near one another by strong, slightly elastic, strap-shaped parts called **ligaments.** Each ligament is anchored at one end to one bone, and at the other end to the other bone. In most joints there are several ligaments spaced out around the joint. Ligaments are strong, but they may sprain or tear under sudden stress.

Top Tips

- Do warm-up exercises for muscles and joints before strenuous exercise.
- Wear suitable protection to avoid excessive flexing or twisting of joints.
- Treat a sprain with rest, and use an ice pack to reduce swelling.
- If there is no improvement in 36–48 hours, or if the pain and stiffness are severe or worsen, always consult a doctor.

Elbow and knee pads protect these joints from hard knocks and falls.

KEEPING JOINTS HEALTHY

Allowing movement

Each joint's design allows a certain range of movement. The ball-and-socket design, such as the hip or shoulder, permits great flexibility but little twisting (rotation of the bone). In the back, each gliding-pivot joint includes a pad of **cartilage,** the intervertebral disc, which is like a cushion between the individual backbones (vertebrae). The joint can flex and twist only slightly, but over the whole backbone this adds up to considerable movement.

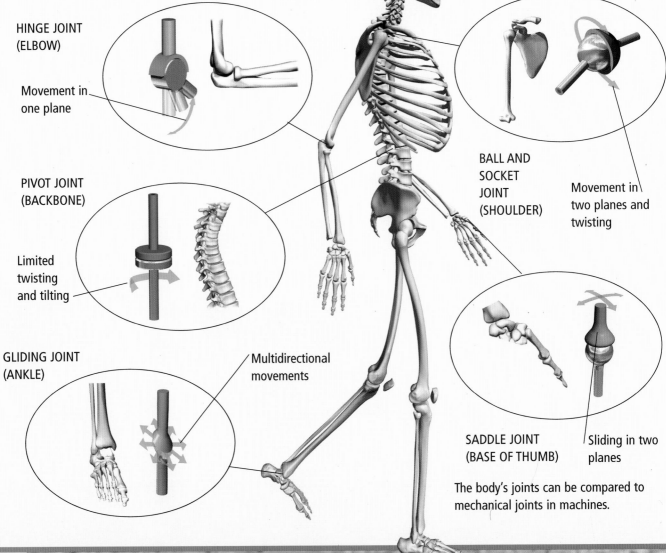

HINGE JOINT
(ELBOW)

Movement in one plane

PIVOT JOINT
(BACKBONE)

Limited twisting and tilting

GLIDING JOINT
(ANKLE)

Multidirectional movements

BALL AND SOCKET JOINT
(SHOULDER)

Movement in two planes and twisting

SADDLE JOINT
(BASE OF THUMB)

Sliding in two planes

The body's joints can be compared to mechanical joints in machines.

Healthy joints

The joints of a young person are more flexible than those of an older person. But old age does not always mean stiff, aching joints. Varied activities and exercises—especially those that are physically not too stressful, like brisk walking, swimming, and yoga—can keep the joints healthy and supple for many years. Sudden twists and turns, in which great stress is put on joints, should generally be avoided.

Gymnasts follow special training routines to keep their muscles strong and their joints supple.

ANIMAL VERSUS HUMAN

Some snakes have more than 200 vertebrae, or individual backbones. So they are very flexible, compared with a human, with 26 vertebrae. A snake's backbone can coil around many times. Some animals have far fewer vertebrae; most frogs, for example, have only eight.

Amazing tools

Our hands and fingers are amazing tools. They can grip and squeeze tightly, spread out wide to rub and stroke, and make the tiniest movements to pick up a pin. This is made possible by their many small bones, joints, and muscles. The wrist has eight bones, known as carpals. The palm has five bones, called metacarpals. And there are three small bones in each finger and two in the thumb, all known as phalanges.

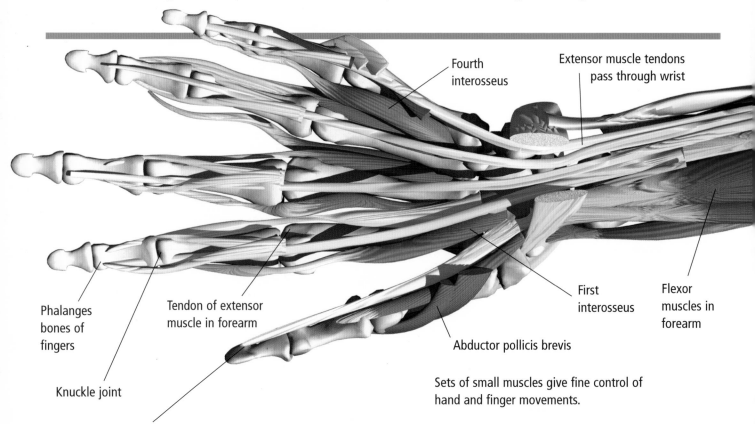

Fourth interosseus

Extensor muscle tendons pass through wrist

Phalanges bones of fingers

Knuckle joint

Tendon of extensor muscle in forearm

Tendon joins to thumb tip

Abductor pollicis brevis

First interosseus

Flexor muscles in forearm

Sets of small muscles give fine control of hand and finger movements.

Moving the hand

Each hand contains about 15 small muscles that move the thumb and fingers at their joints, called knuckles. In particular, they wiggle the fingers from side to side at their knuckle joints with the palm. There are also six large muscles in the forearm that move the fingers. They have very long **tendons** that pass through the wrist and join to the fingers along their length. These mainly bend and straighten the fingers.

Precision and power

The human hand is so useful partly because it has a thumb. This can "oppose" the fingers, when the tip of the thumb touches the tip of each finger in turn. No other animal can do this. It gives us the precision grip to pick up something as small as a grain of rice very delicately, using the thumb and any other finger. It can also create the power grip, where the thumb and fingers wrap around each side of an object, such as when holding a glass.

ANIMAL VERSUS HUMAN

An orangutan has very long fingers but a short thumb. It can only hold things with a hooklike grip. It hangs from its hands as it swings through the trees.

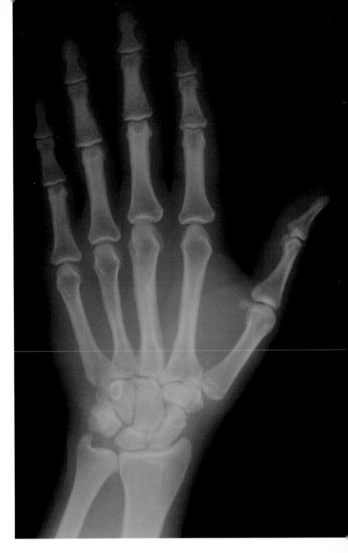

An X ray of an adult human wrist and hand shows the carpal (wrist), metacarpal (palm), and phalanges (finger) bones.

Top Tips

Muscles that are used too much or too suddenly get tired or fatigued. They become weak and begin to shake. In the hand, this makes delicate movements difficult. Practice usually helps, as does taking a break to relax, stretch, and move the fingers in other directions.

A range of movements

There are only three bones in the arm: the humerus in the upper part, and the radius and ulna, which lie alongside each other, in the lower part or forearm. Yet the arm can reach up, forward, down, and even around the back. This is due mainly to the very wide range of motion at the shoulder joint, the more limited bending of the elbow, and also "rotation." This happens when bones twist, or rotate. The wrist may seem more flexible because the hand can bend forward and backward, and can twist around almost in a circle. However, the twisting actually happens all along the arm.

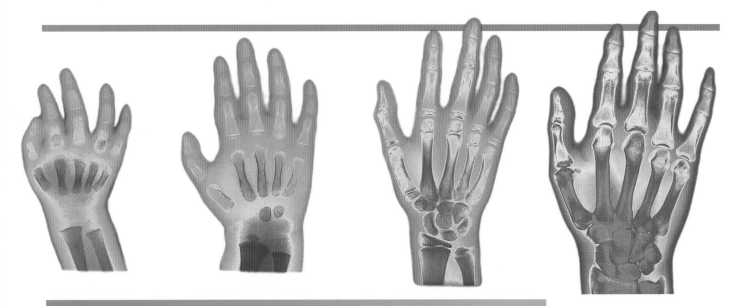

Try this!

Hold your arm out straight in front, palm up. Twist it so the palm turns to face down. Keep going and see how the hand can turn almost in a full circle, so the palm nearly faces upward again. Now, do this while holding your forearm firmly, halfway along, with your other hand. The palm turns much less because the only twisting motion is at the wrist. In the first case, the whole arm was involved, as its long bones twisted along their lengths.

This series of X-ray pictures shows a baby's hand growing into an adult hand. The skeleton in the wrist and hand forms first as cartilage and gradually hardens into bone, here colored blue.

Flexible versus stable

The shoulder is a ball-and-socket synovial joint (see page 34). The ball-shaped upper end of the humerus bone fits into a saucer-shaped socket formed by the shoulder blade and the collarbone. This socket is shallow to allow the arm its amazingly wide range of movements. But the benefit of being more flexible has the drawback of being less stable.

The shoulder's exceptional range of movement is shown well during gymnastic exercises such as the rings.

This means the shoulder joint is sometimes damaged or even pulled apart by too much sudden force, which is called dislocation.

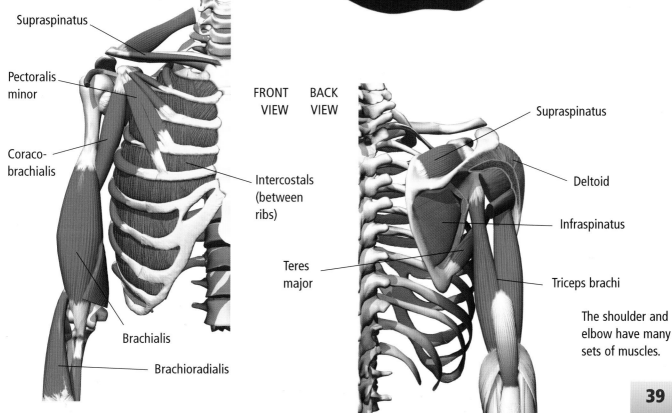

Supraspinatus

Pectoralis minor

Coraco-brachialis

Brachialis

Brachioradialis

FRONT VIEW   BACK VIEW

Intercostals (between ribs)

Teres major

Supraspinatus

Deltoid

Infraspinatus

Triceps brachi

The shoulder and elbow have many sets of muscles.

Differently designed

The leg and foot have almost the same number of bones and muscles as do the arm and hand. But they are designed less for being flexible and more for carrying the body's weight. The hip is a ball-and-socket synovial joint, like the shoulder. But the bowl-like socket is deeper than the socket in the shoulder. This means the leg has a smaller range of movements than the arm. However the hip joint is much stronger and more stable or secure, and less likely to dislocate (come apart).

The power of the leg muscles can propel the whole body more than six feet (two meters) off the ground.

Big and unusual

The biggest single joint in the body is the knee. It is unusual in two ways. It has **ligaments** inside it and around it. There are two inner ligaments between the bones, which are called the cruciate ligaments. Cruciate means cross shaped and these ligaments form a cross or X shape. The knee also has two extra cushionlike pieces of **cartilage** that "float" in the joint between the bone ends. These are crescent- or moon-shaped and called menisci. People such as basketball players and skiers who move quickly and then stop, and twist and turn while moving quickly, put great stress on their knees. They may suffer "cruciate trouble" or "cartilage (meniscus) problems." The hip and leg also have the body's largest muscle. This is the gluteus maximus, which forms part of the buttocks. It pulls the thigh back as we jump and leap.

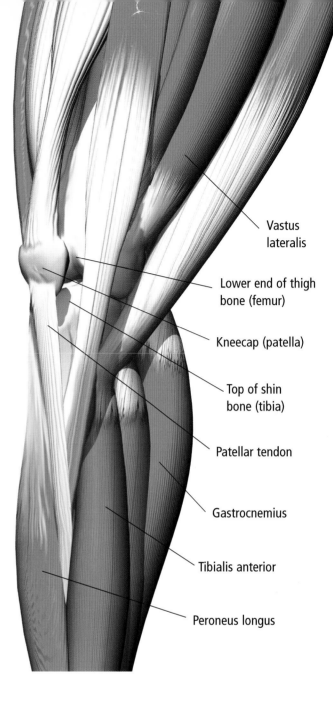

Vastus lateralis

Lower end of thigh bone (femur)

Kneecap (patella)

Top of shin bone (tibia)

Patellar tendon

Gastrocnemius

Tibialis anterior

Peroneus longus

Top Tips

A cramp is a very painful tensing or contraction of a muscle, which feels hard and "knotted." Cramps tend to affect muscles that are used suddenly after long periods of inactivity. The remedy is to stretch the muscle gently by moving the body part and to massage it. However, medical advice is needed for cramps that occur frequently or continue for long periods.

In the knee, the rounded knuckle-like lower end of the femur (thigh bone) fits into the slightly dished top of the tibia (shin bone). The kneecap, or patella, is an unusual bone because it is entirely inside a large tendon, called the patellar tendon. It protects the knee joint at the front.

A tower of strength

The backbone or spine is the main "girder" or "tower" of the body, holding up the head, arms, and torso (central body). It is not one bone, but a chainlike row of 26 bones known as vertebrae. There are 7 vertebrae in the neck region, 12 in the chest (each one is joined to a pair of ribs), 5 in the lower back, one in the hip region (joined to the hip bones), and one small "tail" bone at the lower end. A tunnel runs through the whole backbone. Inside it, well protected, is the body's main nerve: the spinal cord.

Back muscles

Each vertebra has long rodlike extensions called neural spines or processes. These are anchor points where muscles are attached. About 25 sets of long, slim muscles run up and down the backbone, overlapping one another. They join to different sets of vertebrae and link the backbone to the head, shoulders, ribs, and hips. These vertebral muscles give the whole backbone great strength. They also hold the shoulders and hips steady as the arms and legs move.

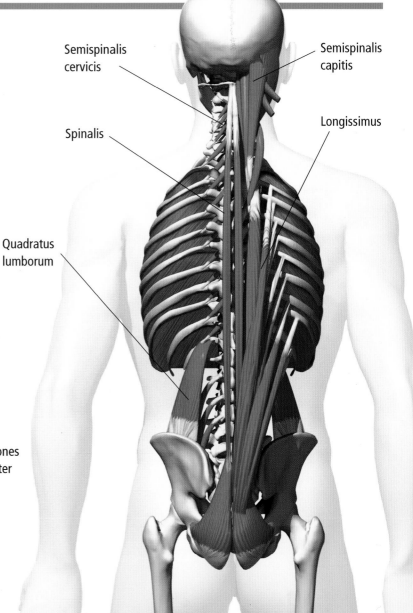

Semispinalis cervicis

Semispinalis capitis

Spinalis

Longissimus

Quadratus lumborum

The cartilage pad, or disc, between each pair of bones in the back, is very strong and tough. It has an outer layer made of stringy fibers, and a slightly more flexible inner layer, or center, almost like stiff jelly. Sets of long back muscles hold the back upright when standing and allow it to bend and twist.

Joints in the back

The vertebral bones have specialized joints. Each has a pad of **cartilage** between its two vertebrae that works like a cushion to absorb knocks and jolts and to let the bones move and tilt slightly. The pad is called the intervertebral disc (see page 34). The disc and the joint's structure allow the two bones to move only slightly in relation to each other. But along the whole backbone, these small movements add up, so the back can bend almost "double" in a U shape.

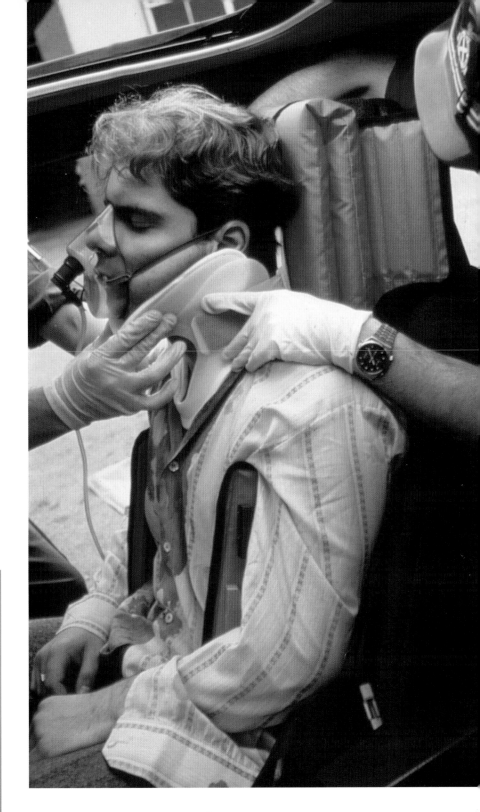

A neck injury may be very serious because of the risk of damage to the spinal cord, which carries nerve signals between brain and body. A neck guard or stabilizer is carefully fitted to hold and support the head during transport to a hospital.

Try this!

Stand up straight, then slowly and carefully, bend your back to the front, side, and back. (Do not strain it.) Which direction is easiest and most flexible? The joints between the vertebrae also allow twisting, so you can keep your feet still but turn around so your head can look backward.

JOINT PROBLEMS

Back strain

Everyday actions such as walking, jogging, and lifting rarely stress the joints. One exception is the back. A back strain is more likely if a person lifts a heavy load by leaning over and bending the back, and perhaps twisting as well, rather than by bending at the hips and knees. Sometimes one of the pads or discs between two vertebrae gets squeezed so much, that it bulges at a weak point in its outer layer and presses on a nearby nerve, causing great pain. The bulge is called a prolapsed (or "slipped") disc.

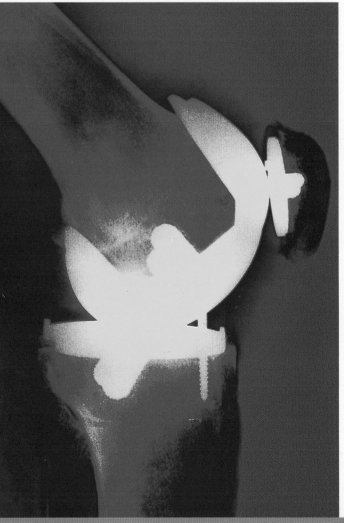

Arthritis

The scientific name for a joint is an arthrosis. The main problems that affect joints, producing pain and swelling, are known as arthritis. There are several types. In osteoarthritis, a joint becomes worn and the smooth **cartilage** in the joint becomes rough and flaky. This is made more likely by old age, too much stress on the joints over the years, and previous injuries. The joints are stiff and achy, especially in the morning.

Many types of artificial joints, such as this knee, are based on the design of the real joint within the body and allow a similar range of movements.

Rheumatoid arthritis

Rheumatoid arthritis is a complicated disease in which the body's immune system, which is supposed to attack invading germs, mistakenly attacks parts of the body itself. This is known as an autoimmune problem. The attacked joints become swollen, painful, stiff, and deformed with lumps. In younger people rheumatoid arthritis is more common than osteoarthritis but it is still a rare condition.

Treatments

Many kinds of medicinal drugs can help different forms of arthritis. So can an operation either to treat the affected parts or to replace them with an artificial joint made of special, hard-wearing plastic and metal.

Healthy muscles and bones

The body's musculoskeletal system is designed for movement and activity. But unsuitable activity and excessive strain can lead to problems, and so can underuse of the system due to inactivity.

MICRO BODY

The cartilage in a joint affected by osteoarthritis is rough, pitted, and crumbly, rather than smooth and slightly flexible.

Experts such as coaches and personal trainers can give advice about keeping the right balance of activities.

Swimming allows the body to be active while supported by water, so it is easier on the musculoskeletal system.

GLOSSARY

actin one of the two main substances shaped as long, thin filaments that, with myosin, is grouped in bundles to form a muscle fibril and that slides past filaments of myosin to make a muscle contract

antagonistic to work against or oppose, as in antagonistic muscle partners attached to one bone, which pull the bone in different or opposite ways

bone marrow soft, jellylike substance in the middle of some bones

calcium important mineral for the body, which in crystal form gives strength and hardness to bones and teeth and keeps other parts of the body, such as nerves, healthy

cancellous (spongy) bone fairly strong but also lightweight, honeycomb-type of bone that forms the middle layer of most bones

cardiac muscle type of muscle that forms the walls of the heart

cartilage strong, tough, lightweight, fairly stiff but slightly flexible substance that makes up structural parts of the body such as inside the nose and ears and that also covers the ends of bones in most types of joints

cell single unit or "building block" of life. The human body is made of billions of cells of many different kinds.

collagen important structural substance in the body; a protein made of many tiny, strong, tough fibers that occurs in the skin, tendons, and many other parts of the body

compact (hard) bone strong, hard, dense type of bone that forms the outer layer or "shell" of most bones, around the less strong cancellous (spongy) layer

contract to pull together; action in a muscle when it tenses and pulls and becomes shorter

hormones natural body chemicals made by parts called endocrine glands that circulate in blood and control many processes such as growth, the use of energy, water balance, and the formation of urine

ligament strong, slightly stretchy, usually strap-shaped part that holds two bones together at a joint to limit their movements and stop them from coming apart

muscle fibers long, thin, thread-shaped parts (myofibers) that are grouped in bundles to make up the bulk of a muscle

muscle fibrils long, thin, thread-shaped parts (myofibrils) that are grouped in bundles to make up the bulk of a muscle fiber

myosin one of the two main substances shaped as long, thin filaments that, with actin, is grouped in bundles to form a muscle fibril and that slides past filaments of actin to make a muscle contract

oxygen gas making up one-fifth of air. Oxygen has no color, taste, or smell, but is vital for breaking down nutrients inside the body to obtain energy for life processes.

peristalsis wavelike, squeezing motion of muscles, especially where they form a tube or bag and squeeze to move along the contents

phosphate mineral made from the substances phosphorus and oxygen, which in crystal form helps give strength and hardness to bones and teeth

relax to be in a resting state; no longer tense and pulling, but becomes floppy and can be pulled longer or stretched

FURTHER INFORMATION

skeletal muscle type of muscle that is mostly joined to the bones of the skeleton, and that is voluntary, able to be moved at will (rather than working automatically without conscious will), and that have tiny stripes or striations when seen under the microscope. Also called a striped muscle.

skeleton all of the body's bones and also the supporting parts made of cartilage

tendon very strong, tough, fibrous, ropelike part where a muscle tapers thinner and anchors to a bone or to another muscle

visceral muscle type of muscle that is mostly deep within the body, especially in the chest and abdomen, but is not joined to the bones of the skeleton, that is involuntary (working automatically without conscious will), and that looks smooth under the microscope because it lacks tiny stripes or striations. Also called a smooth muscle.

vitamin naturally occurring substance either made by the body or taken up in food, that is needed to keep the body healthy and avoid illness

BOOKS

Ballard, Carol. *Bones.* Chicago: Heinemann, 2003.

Ballard, Carol. *Muscles.* Chicago: Heinemann, 2003.

Gardner, Robert. *Health Science Projects About Anatomy and Physiology.* Berkeley Heights, N.J.: Enslow, 2001.

Walker, Richard. *A Guide to the Human Body: A Photographic Journey through the Human Body.* New York: Dorling Kindersley, 2001.

ORGANIZATIONS

American Spinal Injury Association
2020 Peachtree Road NW
Atlanta, GA 30309-1402
(404) 355-9772
www.asia-spinalinjury.org

Arthritis Foundation
P.O. Box 7669
Atlanta, GA 30357
(800) 283-7800
www.arthritis.org

Muscular Dystrophy Association
www.mdusa.org

National Osteoporosis Foundation
1232 22nd Street NW
Washington, D.C. 20037-1292
(202) 223-2226
www.nof.org

INDEX